The Mentor

The Mentor

The Mentor

ELIZABETH SIMON

To order additional copies of this book, contact:
Xlibris
844-714-8691
www.Xlibris.com
Orders@Xlibris.com
816101

Contents

Contents

CHAPTER 1

The Conditional Release

I DECIDED TO write this book to let go of the past. I feel people would not let me let it go but I need to. In 2004, I filed civil action under section 1983 from Calcasieu Correction Center. The federal Judge would not let me precede In Forma Pauperis and said I had to pay the $150.00 filing fee. I elected to have it taken out of my commissary funds. I rarely got commissary funds so I thought it would go away. Here it is June 9, 2020 and I go to the jail to pay the remaining balance of $54.69 on my commissary which was the remaining court fee.

I was found Not Guilty by Reason of Insanity on September 29, 2003. So I filed suit because they would not release me from jail. There was a state agency called Community Forensics that said I could not be released because I did not have housing and mental health treatment. I had basically severed all family ties. I seldom got commissary or a letter from family. My Uncle always sent a little something to me. I did get something from my family but it was not the support most of the inmates had. Unfortunately no one would take me in; I had nowhere to go, so I cooperated with the Community Forensics, a man that was very kind. He was replaced 5 years later by a woman that was very difficult. After the suit was filed and it was learned the federal government had a judgment against the Community Forensics or the jail for holding people in jail without treatment for lengthy periods of time. In fact jails are not hospitals, which is where the mentally ill needs to be. They claimed they had no room at the hospital. Louisiana has two state mental hospitals. Mississippi has less population and they have 5 state mental hospitals. Community Forensics presented me with a Conditional Release. I agreed to it as I felt I could do the 5 years' probation. What I failed to realize that it said yearly contradictory hearings until I was found able. It was twelve years' probation and they did not recommend release, but the Judge decided to release me from probation. To this day, I don't know what I was doing to make them feel unsafe. It was like over time with the right treatment I got better. I didn't break the law. I never knew what the outcome of my civil suit against the jail was since I was released August 1, 2005.

I live an ordinary life in a small town. Everyone knows what I did and the people I did it too. I can only say I'm sorry so many times. For all the years that I had to go to court, only one victim and her family was present in court. She said I deprived her of a quality of life, but truthfully I did not know if she was a good student or had a desire to go to college or even to have a good future. I do know I did not know it was my niece. I did not know who I had shot at the time. I was married to that family for 14 years. It was tragic for me because I felt my feelings for my ex-husband was coupled with his father being murdered on March 1, 1980. I felt sorry for him. I felt he did not really want me but just needed somebody. His father's killer was never found and I feel detectives should have looked more closely at the family for an answer to the killing. The family bickered all the time over property and wrote memo's on what to tell people about the murder. I accompanied my husband on many trips home and witnessed firsthand, all of the family having to sign papers to dispose of property. In 1980, the ex-husband told me his daddy had a mistress, whose boyfriend caught them and then, he told me his father was out gambling. One time he said they knew who killed his father and they got even. He also said he was found with a lot of money, so it wasn't robbery. The newspaper said it was blunt force trauma. I asked to look at the evidence and wondered if I might know something. The police never took me serious. I filed for divorce in April 1994 after my brother Michael was shot and killed by his wife. All the years of verbal and emotional abuse, I had enough. I felt the ex-husband would eventually kill me. He did weird stuff like sleep with a knife on the window sill. One morning he was eating an apple with the knife and getting in his truck. It was still dark but morning and I walked to get the paper. He ran me down with the truck but I only got scrapes and bruises. I called the Sheriff, but decided not to press charges and signed a release not to prosecute. I did not earn enough to be the breadwinner and he definitely would have been convicted. On another occassion I called the cops and the deputy issued a ticket for simple battery. We left the family home and when we returned the next day he was asked to leave the family home. After filing divorce papers and getting custody of the kids. The ex-husband went to trial and was convicted of simple battery. My only daughter testified but later in life said she was sorry she ever did this. He spent a day and a half in jail. But I felt all his fury with over 30 police reports filed because of vandalism to our home and my car. I struggled with my mental illness and felt better when he left. It wasn't long after he moved to Pennsylvania and we moved back to Lake Charles, LA. We had lived in Baton Rouge, LA and had a good life. We sold our house and split the profits. I felt depressed the majority of the marriage but was able to do my motherly duties. I loved my three children and after their father was gone, they all got attitudes but we made the best of life.

The ex-husband filed for sole custody and won in court in 1998. The children were being place in his custody in Pennsylvania. The court ordered me to fly them in from Pennsylvania on certain holidays. The Judge literally severed our relationship as I had no income to afford the extravagant custody plan. As the months went by I returned to college. I filed civil suits in US District Court which I lost interest in. I lived with my mother and two brothers. It wasn't long after that that day came May 30, 2001. In a rage after taking all I could take I took my gun and shot up North Lake Charles.

CHAPTER 2

The Special Housing Unit

I WAS IN isolation for an accumulation of months equaling one year. Most people feel isolation should be ended as being inhumane. I felt it was a good place. A place where I could think read my bible and pray. I spent my time singing R&B and gospel. Nobody cared that I couldn't sing or if it sounded good. The most of the time I was incarcerated I had few visitors, few comforts, and definitely no freedoms. I had never been to jail in my life. I did not know what to expect. But I learned if you shut up and mind your business people leave you alone. This is how it is I thought of life in the SHU (special housing unit) also called the hole. The worst that could happen is the mental state would go beyond insane. Insane that is what the Sanity Commission said. They said at the time of the crime spree I did not know right from wrong. I never talked to a detective or policeman concerning what happened. I only talked to doctors. I was in a dark place and full of anger. I had time to think about what I did. I never had time to prepare to speak with the psychiatrist. They had ways of detecting deception and it wasn't an act.

I was in cell number 608, the window would not open, and the male inmates would walk up to the window eyeing me in my cell. I observed on one occasion when I had a cell mate that she flashed her breast and got a lit cigarette. I got a shower twice per week and a smoke break that may or may not come. I often shared my tobacco with the other inmates. One time we were so mellow, I would go out to recreation with the guys. When I was at smoke break I talked to someone through the window. I never knew his name or what he looked like.

One day, I was in my cell and the guy next to me started calling asking if I was the lady that shot up those people? I responded, yes it was me. I ask him why he was in there. All he said was he got in a fight in the dorm. He shared a scripture. I sat down by the toilet and noticed a vent that you could see in the next cell. It was why I could hear him so well. I looked to see if I could see. All I could see was the floor. He asked me, if I was 42 and I said yes. I asked him for the scripture, and he said, "Love covers a multitude of sins". He said, you should pray for love.

Chow comes at the same time every day, so the guards would yell chow. Then you would hear the door flaps opening. On one occasion, I did not want to eat. So when he opened the slot I said I'm not hungry. The trustee shoved the tray in and I shoved the tray back. Then I placed my hand on the flap and the guard kicks the flap slamming my hand in the door. I screamed and looked at my hand all purple and bruised. I press the button for help and eventually a guard came and suggested I did it to myself. They took a statement and gave me ice and some pills.

On another occasion, I realized I was the only female housed in the section with 1500 men. The security system malfunctioned and the doors opened. I walked out of the cell and stood in the hallway. The deputy walked down the hall and handcuffed me and escorted me to one of the meeting rooms where she waited for hours while they repaired the computer.

In time, they kicked me out the SHU and back into general population with 30 other women. Most of them drug addicts, child molesters, drug dealers and many of them sexually abused as children. I will be able to go to church and anger management. In my case it should be rage management. I would not sit with the gay people and they left me alone too. In time, I did sit and talk with certain inmates. Many confided they had been sexual abused as children. Sometimes by a step father, a mother's boyfriend, an uncle, a grandfather or some family connection. It was heartbreaking I could relate to the sexual abuse. I was only 15 years old when someone broke into our home and tried to rape me in my room. I had for a few nights heard noises, like someone was trying to get in. That night, I turned my light on and I lay there with my eyes closed. I heard someone walk across the room. When I opened my eyes I saw him covering his face. He dove on me and I fought him and screamed. I bit his hand so hard. When they kicked my door in, he ran off, and one of my brother's ran after him. The man was never arrested. My dad had me brought to the police station and talk to a young man. I asked him to see his hands. They were smooth and my attacker's hands were rough. They never found who attacked me. I learned that we suffered some of the same things. I wasn't in general population long before I ended back in the SHU.

While in 600 block, I found a book about addiction and bondage. Although I never abused drugs or was addicted I sat around with my two brothers drinking beer. I found a section on forgiveness in the book. The instructions in the book were write down the names of everyone that has hurt you and pray that you forgive them. I felt that really helped. I came up with 14 names and began to relive the abuse I suffered. One by one, I began to heal as she released that person from what they did to me. I began to think when it all started. My mother described being pregnant with Pete whose real name is Terrance. She said she had to carry him a lot and that he hurt her back. That after having Pete she had back surgery. He was born in December 1957 and I was born in May of 1959. Apparently, she got pregnant the same year she had back surgery. That is an abuse in its self. I can't believe my dad who eventually had back surgery and he put his big self on her and made me. That would make anyone wonder if they were welcome or a wanted baby. My thoughts were on the painkillers, morphine, anesthesia and drugs used during the surgery. My father appetite for sex being a person who had already fathered seven children, not waiting until she was out of a body cast to have sex. The scar that I saw was from her neck down her back. My mother often spoke about when she went in to the hospital to get her off opioids'. I prayed that every bad feeling I had toward my parents be forgiven. This doesn't mean I hated them it means they did things as parents that we endured that were not what parents should do. My father's drunken rages when he would burst in the house and wake us up for an occasional lecture. His strictness that applied to us, his children, but not to him and his mistress who became his wife later on.

I was always there for my mother. I worked and brought income into the house. When I got pregnant with my first child, she told me she was not a babysitter. I asked my neighbor to babysit and she did. Then I sent him to daycare, they would pick him up and drop him off. Mom only had to watch him an hour. Then, me ex-husband, who was not the father would pick him up and bring him to our apartment. It wasn't difficult to coordinate home and work. When it was time for my parents' divorce I went with my mother to California and she was awarded the house and some apartments. They divorced after all. Even after I married and was living in Baton Rouge, I always made sure she had. My sister Francine contributed too. Michael helped as much as he could. He sometimes lived with her.

While in the SHU, you could hear every sound. I would wait for chow some days. One day I was just waiting on chow and a note came and as the trustee thrust the tray through something fell. I look down and saw a pack of bugler and a cigarette lighter. A man from my old neighborhood was kind to me. The note said he was sending a radio and some cookies later. She anticipated the crew picking up the trays so she could smoke. After an hour the crew came and picked up the trays. From that time on I was careful not to be caught with the lighter and the tobacco. I had cigarettes in my locker but not a lighter. Although, the jail allows one hour recreation we didn't always get that smoke break outside. My property was kept in a locker down the hall. I rolled the cigarette and sat on the floor by the toilet and smoked.

I appreciated when the female deputies would come and let me shower. They would search for contraband but they never found it. I had the lighter under my breast and the tobacco in my thermal underwear. They searched the room and they patted me down. Sometimes I think they knew and just felt sorry for me being in isolation without committing any offense. Whatever the case may be they never caught me. Everybody shared the same shower and sometimes the windows were not covered and the guys watched me go down the hall.

I had settled down one evening and the door opens and there was standing an elderly deputy who was tall and stocky. Here's your radio and hands me a paper bag with cookies. I felt so much appreciation to Waldron and the deputy. Waldron came from a prominent family and had spent most of his life in and out of jail. He was Phillips best friend and I guess that friendship still existed.

I had so many arguments about this same guy and he comes through for me like a hero in jail.

It wasn't long before the lights went out on the cell that had 15 foot ceilings and was about 8 feet by 12 feet. I laid there listening to my radio and eating cookies.

CHAPTER 3

My Childhood

I FOUND WAYS to amuse myself in isolation. I certainly had enough time to think. I began thinking about my early years of childhood. I remembered the house we lived in at 18 Bondview Street. It was a dead end street on a hill below Folsom Street in San Francisco, California. I remembered sharing a space underneath the stairs of our two stories home with Francine. I would hide underneath my bed when my parents would fight.

One afternoon I was playing on the sidewalk with my little brother. I saw the light colored yellow station wagon parked up the street. I went inside and I did not get my little brother. I was only two years old. My father, Herbert walks into the house holding my little brother, who had blood streaming from his head and body. The woman in the station wagon was a drunk driver who hit my little brother saying she thought it was a branch. She was white we were black. There were no drunken driving laws at that time which was about 1961.

Another childhood memory was when my legs went numb for no reason. I was playing in the kitchen and my legs just gave out and I fell in a split. I was taken to the hospital. They thought it was polio but then my feeling came back just as mysteriously as it had stopped. I felt the pain of being number eight out of nine children. Sometimes it seemed there was not enough love to go around. Michael and Ronald (who we call Googie) put me in a tire and sent me down the hill. Then my brothers would put me in a blanket and throw me in the air. It was fun hanging out with the boys. I felt they are the reason I am so tough.

I had a moment thinking of my older sister who sent me commissary funds a couple of times. When she sent the funds it was a lot. But I would run up my indigent account and when they finally got around to giving me medicine they took five dollars out for each prescription and I got the balance. My older sister had brown and blond hair with hazel eyes. She was beautiful and she was a child that had favor with both parents. It was her that knew all the family secrets. She tried to be supportive but the pain of what I did was too much for her. Her little sister that she thought she knew and loved. I was now the pin cushion for her fiery darts.

My parents always opened their doors to family. Whoever wanted to come to California to escape racism in the South was welcome. So the family was a big family that included Uncles and Aunts, cousins, and friends.

I felt I was at the mercy of my older brothers and sisters. They teased me calling me liver lips, black bitch, gu gu and I was made to feel ugly. Then my dad would add fuel to the fire saying I was for Pete the motorcycle driver that lived down the street. I am so glad they have DNA because I am my dad's child according to 23 and me. My parents did not want a divorce because they were Catholic. So they lived in misery fighting all the time. Something I was not going to do. Francine became a better sister in later years. We would go everywhere together. We attended church at Sacred Heart and to Walkers Recreation Center to hang out or learn ceramics. She had her girlfriends who also came up with some good stuff. I learned twirling, jacks and all kinds of games. In our teen years, my older sister and I got in fights. My sisters went to the same junior high and high school that I was going to go to. Teachers judged me by the things that they did. My sisters took home economics so I took home economics. I especially liked sewing. In junior high the Pearl Watson Junior High Pageant we were to model the clothes we made. I remember well and will never forget an evening I told my older sister it was time for me to use the bathroom that I was in the pageant not her. She called me a ho short for whore... I had made an afro and modeled my pant set my feelings crushed because I was called something that labeled me a whore. My mom fueled this because she cornered me and asked me if I was using tampons. I said yes. She said whores use this. In spite of being labeled a whore I had my virginity a long time. Even after I married she still called me a ho. I used tampons because I was becoming an athlete. The pads were too bulky and annoying to wear.

When my older sister was 16 years old she went to live with my dad and his mistress. This hurt my Mom. My dad had opened another store on the corner of Shattuck and Commercial. Rose was the older sister, then I had three older sisters, Rose and my older sister shared a room. I had another sister; she and I shared a room. He also had a washerteria with apartments on top. Rose and my older sister had some kind of issue with my brothers. There were two sisters who lived with my dad's mistress and my dad. In 1976 my dad shut down his business and skipped town with his mistress and my older sister. Thank God he left Rose with us. If it were not for Rose we would not have survive this change in our life. He abandoned the three younger children, who were all in high school. .

Rose was sometimes in charge because the family used a democratic system that the oldest was always in charge. Rose was a sickly child. At the age of 12 she was hit by a taxi cab while riding on the back of a bike driven by Pete. It was learned at that time she had scoliosis. This developed into a hump on her back. We were senseless and called her hunchback. That was until one day a woman heard me say it and told me it was cruel and to respect her feelings. It was said to me with a mature, dignified, and forceful manner. I never called her that again. Rose went to New Orleans, LA to have back surgery. She was given an iron brace to wear. At night, Rose was bob and bounce all night in the bed that has a metal box spring for the mattress base. She would play the radio loud all night. This went on every night. It was Rose's strength that I learned from. She was courageous and beautiful with long black silky hair. She wanted to be a nun and was turned down because they did not take people with disabilities. She stood for everything good. She developed a drinking problem. I didn't blame her for this, when I saw what she went through. Whereas Francine was calling me a whore, Rose was telling me I were beautiful. Rose taught me how to drive. Rose taught me how to count money and assist customers in our dad's grocery store. If I could rename Rose her name would surely be Love because that is what she was.

After, my father and his mistress skipped town without paying a single bill or liquidating his assets. They left all businesses and everything and just left for San Francisco to live in our old house on Bonview Street. My older sister called me and convinced me to come and visit. My mother was so angry that I was going to stay with my dad in California. It was a mistake and I should have known that he would not really want me there. One evening my dad drunk too many or probably popped painkillers. It was 12 am and he began hollering at my older sister for coming in late and not making curfew. He went upstairs and began throwing her clothes out of the window. He was yelling every night; she comes in at two or three in the morning. I want you out of here, get out of my house. I called my uncle to come get me and told him I wanted to go back to Louisiana. I didn't last a month in San Francisco. It was at the time Harvey Milk was shot and the gay people held protest and we were told to stay inside. I did not know much about homosexuality, I got the impression they were bad people. We always saw gay people on Enterprise Blvd. in Lake Charles, LA. It was a bad street where prostitutes stood out in the open and it had lots of night clubs. It no longer exists today. Well my opinion of gay people changed after being incarcerated. I learned people are human and I have no right to judge or discriminate. In fact, I had one woman tell me I was always kind to her, so I know I changed my heart before I left jail.

My older sister and I did spend a lot of time together as children. If she went to the nightclub, even though she was underage, she brought me with her and encouraged me to talk to older guys. There was no love interest there. My older sister really did not know me and had left our home on Jackson Street in 1976. I went to San Francisco in 1977 for one month. I saw her in 1982 after I married. I saw her in 1989 than in again in 1995. I winced as I remembered the 1995 visit when my older sister began arguing with her over some pictures. She tried to hit me, while her husband stepped in and said lets go. Some people will never change. My older sister began yelling Fuck you, Fuck you. She found me, alone and vulnerable and instead of being supportive she joined the ex-husband to get custody of our children. The Community Forensics team relied heavily on information about my background that came from her and honestly she could provide nothing solid about my past.

As I knelt on my knees and prayed for forgiveness of my sisters, for name calling, physical abuse and insults and just being a bad influence. I prayed to God to forgive my sister and brother Ronald for giving evidence to the D.A. that they found in writings in my room. It was my second oldest sister that started me smoking cigarettes. When you really think about it I did not know my sister much because from 1977 to 1998, I saw my sister about 4 times. Of course we talked on the phone but it really was not a close relationship. My older sister did pay my house note when I first separated. After my sister in law shot my oldest brother. My older sister inherited an insurance payment. She said she was doing something for everybody. She gave 1000.00 but later said she loaned it to me.

I prayed to forgive my ex-husband and his family. The years of insults and abusive treatment when we were excluded from his family for gatherings and social events were endured. On one occasion, my son stayed with the ex-husbands older brother and wife. The children gave him Mad Dog 2020 and got my oldest son drunk, they then had him tattooed with a dog. He hid this from me for many years never telling me what they did to him when I let him be in their care.

I continued living in the SHU for months. I read books like The Green Mile, I studied and read my Holy Bible and I prayed God would restore my freedom. One day a letter arrives from my older sister. I received a hundred dollars for my commissary. The letter read, your plea will be changed to Not Guilty by Reason of Insanity and you will not have to be there much longer. She wrote, you shot our brother and you're guilty but you will go free. You shot one man five times!!! You are an animal and a disease. She signed Love. I was shocked and that was not love. I put the letter in an envelope and sent it to the District Attorney. I was angry with my attorney for discussing my case with my sister.

I had a Public Defender that was a conflict attorney. I had the attorney assigned to me recused because he was just too close to our family. Then, another attorney talked with me and he was recused because he was close to the ex-husband's family. Finally, I settled in with an attorney. I regret that I could not allow my neighbor to represent me. We had grown up on Jackson Street with a house between us. My attorney did not accept collect calls. I wrote to him asking if it were true and wanted to know the status of my case. He said he could not confirm that the District Attorney will accept the Not Guilty by Reason of Insanity plea. He said we were able to get your brother's psychiatric medical records and enter them as evidence. It was at the time, I understood because my brother was a paranoid schizophrenic who went in and out of psychiatric hospitals. We could not accept my father left us and began having mental problems at that time. He brutally beat his supervisor at a local paint plant and spent years in Jackson State hospital.

Months passed and I filed grievance after grievance while housed in general population. You could call me a rat. I didn't bother nobody and every once in a while I would like to watch a movie or just watch a program to the end. Every morning we rise to the same old funky lockers and funky smell. The worse thing commissary did was put that old funky smelling perfume on the list. They called me to the door and said put your uniform on. I was brought to the office. My sister Roxann was there. The Captain and the Chaplain was present. They said your mother has passed. He asked me if I had any one I was closed to or if I wanted to be alone. I said I would like to go to isolation. I went back to pack up and holding back my tears. I go on the long walk to Intake. When I get to the prison, I stopped and fell to my knees crying. I howled and I did not care if the deputies saw me. I did not care what they thought and they seem to show no emotion. I stood up and walked to intake. I was put in a cell and I fell to my knees saying my rosary in the dark. The Captain opened the door to check on me and I am crying telling him I was okay.

I was given a choice to go to the funeral or go to the wake. They said my sisters were bringing me clothes. The clothes never came and I went to the wake in my orange prison uniform. There were only a few people there. I went to view the body and pray for my mamma. As I closed my eyes and I am praying I saw her hand reach down to me. I said no, I'm not ready to go. At least I said good bye.

I returned to my cell. I was not given counseling and I just preferred to be alone. When I saw one of my childhood friends I was incarcerated with, again, I told her my mother died. She said how sorry she was because she told everyone I was sent to isolation because I was writing too many grievances.

CHAPTER 4

School Days

THE CAPTAIN OF the women's prison came by and she said we are moving you to intake in the morning. I thought how all the peace and quiet will be gone. But was not surprised because I was upset when I had received my breakfast an inmate walked up to my window and began peering inside. I threw my plate at the window breaking the plate. The deputy came and saw the grits all over the window and got the men's prison Captain. The plate was broken and sharp. The Captain braced up to me and I pushed him. After that, I knew that I would be sent back maybe to isolation and the news of release had been too much for my fragile mind.

I arrive at intake and I am in a better place. The cell faced the recreation area with basketball courts and lots of men. I am housed with male inmates. A man that was famous for shooting up K K's corner. At five in the morning a male inmate would holler if anybody was up? Then, usually breakfast would come. The food was being cooked at the jail and then they changed it and got rid of that process. I missed those big biscuits they had.

I spent my time singing gospel songs I had learned from jail church. Church in jail was made of up lay ministers. They were ordinary people who volunteered to bring the religious services to the inmates. If you're in intake you couldn't go to church. So I made my own church praying and singing. This morning I began singing Troubles in this World. One inmate complained that Mahalia Jackson won't shut up. Then I heard a familiar voice and it was my cousin trying to talk in tongues.

I laid back and fell into a deep sleep and I started out my dreaming about my childhood friend when I was around 5 years old. I met her when our family moved from San Francisco to Lake Charles, LA in about 1962. She lived closest to the railroad. She had a swing in her back yard.

I was playing with her when she asked, "Are you going to school?" I looked across the street at Jackson Street School, and asked you mean over there? She said yes, there's a Head Start coming to the school and you have to have all your shots.

"What's a shot?" I asked.

They take a long needle and stick it in your arm and it hurts and bleeds. I thought, about the pain and hoped I would be able to take the baby aspirins to make it not hurt.

After moving from San Francisco, I had never seen a dark skin person. I am black but we are all light skinned. There was no reason to teach us about different races as we played together as a family and never went into the city much to encounter other races. At the park there were always white people. Now, we are in the South and in a small town that was divided into North Lake Charles for black people and South of Broad Street for white people.

She was the best friend anyone could have. Her granny was nice and so was her grandfather. He worked and granny kept their house clean and always cooked something that smelled so good. I searched Carmen's face for the truth and she was not lying.

I ran home and asked my mamma about school. She said she had got a notice from the school about a program. She said, you have to have your birth certificate and your shot record. As time went by I was taken to get my shot at the Public Health.

I started the Head Start Program started by President Lyndon Johnson in 1965 along with the Food Stamp program.

School was so much fun and we learned so much. The Hokey Pokey and other games were played out on the huge playground. Jackson Street Elementary had grades Head Start to 6th grade. There were some mean girls and I did my best to avoid them. I didn't know but would find out would attend school with the same students all the way to 12th grade.

Time went by and Head Start was going on. I understood that I would have the whole day away from my brother's and sister's. My mamma got all the supplies together including a yellow blanket that she had to cut in half it was so long. I had two blankets, one for home and one for school. The blanket at home got the most usage as Pete would pull me around the house in it and it was a fun game. Then after the game, I looked at the blanket and it had a big black dirt spot. Pete always got me in trouble. Just like one day, Daddy told us to take a nap because mamma was not there. Pete takes a piece of brown bag and lit it and put it in the dresser. The dresser caught on fire and the fire department came. We were spanked but it was Pete that did it.

I was selected to be in a school program. I was to be in a play in front of the school. I had to wear green and white the school colors. I had to get my hair fixed. Also, white tennis shoes and socks. I felt special and a feeling of accomplishment.

Mamma sewed a white skirt and dyed it green. She bought a white blouse and tennis shoes. Even though we owned the grocery store across the street we had problems making ends meet. Mamma taught me the words to Jimmy Crack Corn. All I can remember now is Jimmy Cracked Corn but I don't care because today is a holiday.

It was a big day in the gymnasium at Jackson Street Elementary. The WO Boston High School chorus was there in red robes with white collars. I was in awe of all the students and parents. I had an uneasy feeling but I have to I thought. We lined up on stage and we sang and danced and the crowd loved it. Nothing gratified and her more than to hear the choir sing Wade in the Water and Oh Happy Day. These are songs I will remember for the rest of my life. In today's time WO Boston is gone, Reynaud Junior High gone. But and there is always a but for the good things, the Panther's Den website keeps alumni informed and together.

The school yard was always the center of activity. After school, another large family like ours brought out the baseball equipment. All the kids in the neighborhood headed to the neighborhood school. A block a way was another school. Every afternoon the Washington High School band headed to that school yard to practice. The older kids and adults put up a table to play dominoes or spades. One day there was a big fight and a man got hit over the head with a bottle. The police came and we rarely saw the police in our neighborhood.

The store front always had people on the porch. The store was connected to the house where all nine children and our parents lived. At the schoolyard, they also played horseshoes. There was an awareness of people who suffered from mental illness. There was a man who was very fair skinned who had been burned with acid thrown in his face. There was a woman that walked with a crooked foot. It was said she had been raped. There was Jack Mahoney who was scared of people especially girls. He would run when you called his name. They said he was a veteran and he was shell shot. There was a veteran and his hand shook. He had six children and all the families from that area played at Jackson Street Elementary which was once called First Ward Colored and the school down the street called First Ward White.

The next big fight was when mamma found out about my dad's mistress; for God's sake we had nine kids in our family. There was a case of coke bottles and in the middle of the night we are awakened by our parents screaming and throwing bottles, she called him a moon faced nigger.

If that wasn't enough misery for my mamma, my aunt by marriage went into the store for a beer and after my mamma sold her the beer. The sheriff's came in an arrested mamma for selling liquor so close to the school. She was never the same after that. She went into the hospital for abusing pain pills and she was gone a long time.

I missed her so much. There was no one to comb my kinky hair. Rose tried to comb it and should have been grateful. Then a neighbor stepped in to help our family with my hair condition. No matter how hard my scalp hurt when they combed my hair I did not scream. They washed it and combed it. They pressed it and I liked it. I felt so good and thankful for these new friends who lived on the next block. Then another neighbor stepped in to help prepare meals. We now had the support of the community. As the years went by my father tried to discourage me from pressing my hair with a straightening comb.

I had grown up in the civil rights era. I was in third grade when a girl was crying. I asked her why she was crying. She said Martin Luther King, Jr got killed. I did not know who he was at the time. But he was something like the President John F. Kennedy that was killed. We watched that funeral on TV.

It was in intake, I connected with a guy from the past, my older sister boyfriend from the late 70's. I wished that it would have been me that was his girlfriend I always liked him and I could see him looking at me. He was a kitchen trustee. He didn't bring any cigarettes but he bought good food like sausages, chicken with the bone, fish, and good salads. I welcomed see him every day at recreation time for the guys. A famous inmate that had been locked up for 40 years could be seen jogging and he had a watch. The inmates would ask him what time is it and he responded without hesitation. I learned my mom's house burned down, that meant I had nowhere to go for sure. It was an agonizing loss.

I continued reading my bible. When I was first arrested an old school inmate told me to order a big word Holy Bible and a Faith to Faith. I watched various inmates reading their bible. I was not in the habit of reading it every day. I started using the calendar in the back of the book. I read 4 chapters at a time. When I wasn't using my Holy Bible, I was drawing and playing Solitaire. I must have read that Bible seven times. This was how I spent my days in isolation. I would sing, read, and play cards and draw. It wasn't long before the guy I was writing to got out of jail and his charges were not serious. He began to visit me and I was glad to see him outside of the jail.

About a later, the inmate who would holler every morning before chow, is anybody up, was shot and killed by a police officer in front of Reynaud Middle School after being released. He was mentally ill and homeless.

CHAPTER 5

Hallucinations or Apparitions

I TRIED NOT to think of my crime spree that left my brother dead and three other people wounded with non-life threatening injuries. It was second degree murder and three counts of attempted first degree murder. The Community Forensic doctors said I tried to minimize my crime. I never could figure where they got that from when these were the charges. I felt it should have been manslaughter and aggravated assault. After all it was the first time I offended, but who was I to complain.

I acknowledge I always saw things but then I said I was clairvoyant. I questioned myself whether they were visions or ghosts, or just hallucinations. I can remember the first time I saw something. I was with my dad in San Francisco and we visited this house my Uncle Charles was working on. As I walked into what was a garage, this beautiful lady. I was at the top of the stairs. I climbed the stairs and then started to cry because it was so high. The shining lady picked me up and I floated down to the bottom. I feel that a two; year old doesn't know what is real and what isn't. But this was the first of a supernatural experience or a hallucination.

I thought about my bad feelings toward my brother whom I shot. I loved going to church and was allowed to go to Catechism. The nuns had planned some competitive things for classes. One of the contests was an art contest. I wanted to participate. I first saw nuns in San Francisco, I respected their authority. Our family attended Immaculate Conception and on some days they gave us cinnamon candy rapped in red cellophane paper when we visited. I liked nuns and wanted to become a nun when I grew up.

After moving to Lake Charles, LA we began attending Sacred Heart Church. When I was about 4 years old I started crying in church. A white nun reached down and picked me up and I stopped crying and felt at peace.

As a child I connected these women to good things. They were virgins who dedicated their lives to the Church.

I asked my brother, who later is my victim, to help me draw my picture for the art contest. He was to draw the devil and I was going to draw Jesus telling the devil to leave his children alone. He drew this big devil and I drew Jesus who looked very; small. I thought nothing of it. But the nun asked me if I drew it myself and I lied saying yes and not telling her Pete drew the devil big. I won third place. The nun stopped me and asked me if I drew it alone. I lied and said yes. She said I should not have drawn the devil bigger than Jesus. I understood my mistake and told my brother he drew the devil to big. The nun gave me a small plastic book with the Guardian Angel prayer and a metal.

It wasn't long I was about 9 or 10 when I was looking in the mirror. I saw this beautiful woman with long flowing blue robes and black hair covered with a scarf. Our eyes met and then she was gone. I never told anyone about these things because it wasn't known to me about mental illness.

It was after I married and it was a stormy night. I was in the bedroom on the second floor of our apartment. I awoke to see a thing in our room. It was all in white and had feathers and was holding a sickle. I know what I saw and I was not playing with Ouija boards or Tarot cards or anything of that sort.

In 1988, I remember being depressed after I was fired from a job. I got into a fight with a neighbor. He pushed me and tried to strike me. I had my wisdom teeth pulled and was on Vicodin. I pressed charges of simple battery against him. I began hearing voices out of nowhere. I felt I was in danger. I felt my children were in danger. Somehow I thought I hallucinated because I was on meds for various ailments. I took them all at once. The voices kept saying I will show the world how beautiful you are and then I am going to kill you. The voices I heard said various things I don't remember. This I feel was a hallucination.

Then in the 90's, I was praying the Rosary early one morning before work. When I returned from work and went into my bedroom. There was a huge sphere of light on the wall. I walked up to it and touched it and it definitely didn't shine on my hand. I began covering the windows to block the light, every place where light could come from was covered. The sphere stayed there.

I lay down and went to sleep not aware of what is going on. The door began to shake as if something was trying to get in. I felt myself rise off of the bed. My gold cross around my neck began to rise also. I am not sure if it were a dream and I know it was impossible if it wasn't a dream. I refrained from sharing this with any psychiatrist as they already addressed psychosis in my meds. I never refused the meds.

It was around that time, I was awakened to a man whispering my name. I was too afraid to get up. I went back to sleep as I had no known stalkers and there should not be any reason any man should be whispering my name.

As time went on, I called myself meditating on the floor near my mom's oxygen machine. I had my legs folded and had closed my eyes rolling them up to a point to form a triangle in her mind and began to hum. I counted to 4 as I held my breath.

There was a loud bang and I ran to the window where my brother was sleeping, drunk from beer. I saw that same green devil in the flashing of light from the electric lines. The window rose up and shut down with no one standing on the other side. The lights went out and I realized a transformer burnt up causing the loud bang.

My last vision or hallucination occurred when I was in jail. The women often talked about the Holy Bible when one of them kneeled down and prayed for a sign. The next day we were outside sitting on a tire that was part of the volley ball net poll. I looked up and saw a cross in the sky. It was big, white and fluffy like cotton against the blue sky. Only for a moment before it was covered by another patch of clouds.

I was later moved back to general population. It was just another boring day. You wake up at 6 am for breakfast. After breakfast everyone has to make their beds to jail specifications. This means every bunk must have the sheets tucked in, blankets folded exactly right. There is no sleeping under the bedding until 6 pm. After breakfast also, was the hustle and bustle of cleaning the dorm before 7 am. That's when you can smoke and watch television. It is better known as recreation time. Church was an outlet for me. When it first started out the lay ministers or Mentors would come into the dorms. One inmate complained they were forcing her to be a part of it. Then, Church was moved to the classroom. My first time attending church a woman, from Christian Baptist Church looked at me and said someone is confused your mind is not clear. We are going to pray that your mind is healed. I felt she was talking to me and I did begin thinking better. She shared that she too had been incarcerated and went to the penitentiary. She earned a college degree. She showed her scars where she was beat down. She said she was swing from the bars at the old jail downtown butt naked. She told us how her life was changed through prayer. I attended Church on Sundays, Tuesdays and Fridays. Choir practice was two days out of the week.

CHAPTER 6

The Release from Jail

SOMEHOW, I FOUND my niche in jail after being in isolation for so many times. I became a trustee. I began working as the Paralegal and Librarian. I would assist in filling out forms to submit to court also, for helping inmates check out and return books. I would hand out the forms and later the inmates could request for me to meet with them in the classroom where all the activities took place. I stopped getting in arguments and fights. I had no choice but to take the medicines. I never made a friend in jail or got along with anyone. I was never a part of the street life.

I didn't expect to hear ATW Elizabeth Simon. My time had come. It had been 4 years and 4 months. I looked around and they had racked up all inmates. I did not get a good bye or write to me or anything from any inmate. I packed up and was brought to a waiting area. I was told to change. All I had was a pair of gray sweatpants, white t-shirts, white boxers, white socks in a white laundry bag. I had towels and underwear. I kept every court paper I was ever issued.

The plan in September 2003 was to release me to a day hospital in New Orleans, LA. That never happened and every day from September 2003 until the day of release I waited in anguish to be released. They refused to release me unless I signed a Conditional Release. I signed it without advice of an attorney. It was a good thing I did not go to New Orleans, LA. Six weeks later Hurricane Katrina slammed New Orleans.

I was released to two women from Volunteers of America housing program. I had been interviewed by them earlier as my needs were mental illness and homelessness. I was given my belongings a pair of purple sun glasses, a gold cross and chain, and my driver's license. Everything else I had when I came into jail was kept as evidence. I was not told to pick anything up.

The woman that picked me up was a caseworker with Volunteers of America and I owe her so much for helping me. I thank God until today for her not giving up and throwing in the towel where I was concerned. She quit working with us but not before getting me into an apartment of my own at Lake Villa Assisted Living.

On the first day, Tina began explaining the rules. She said someone will come and give you your meds twice per day. The medication will be locked up in your unit. You will go to the drop in center every day. The van will pick you up in the mornings and take you downtown. There will be used clothing and a meal. We will apply for emergency food stamps. We have to report to Probation and Parole.

From that point on, she was my caseworker. She had everything worked out and accompanied me to every appointment and sat in the appointment. .

I called my boyfriend to let him know I was released. He asked me what I wanted. I said Churches Fried Chicken and some beauty supplies. We spent the night alone

I was paired with a roommate who came with a lot of boxes of clothes and she was an alcoholic. We were all called into a meeting. It was announced that Hurricane Katrina had struck in New Orleans on August 29, 2005. It was a catastrophic hurricane that displaced residence all across America. They said there was a hurricane brewing and we need information in order to evacuate. When it was my turn to answer questions. I had no next of kin and no support from any of my family. Point blank, I told them I have no family was told if the hurricane strikes we will have to live in a shelter for three weeks.

On September 23, 2005, the residents packed and loaded up into vans and head for places unknown.

The woman, who was my roommate, was traveling in another van. I was hoping we would be separated the entire trip. I was relieved to know that. First stop were Elton, LA. Then in the morning we left for Monroe LA. September 24th, 2005 Hurricane Rita made landfall in Lake Charles, LA. Hurricane Rita showed no mercy as she tore up Lake Charles, LA.

We stayed there a week and then said our goodbyes. We headed for Baton Rouge, LA. We were welcomed at an Assisted Living Facility. I was housed with two other women.

I had a passion for Baton Rouge because this is where I married and raised my children. It felt good being in a familiar place. Before leaving we said our good byes again but not leaving until we filled out our FEMA papers for being displaced.

We make it home and the apartment complex was damaged and a huge oak tree was a few feet from the entrance. The oak tree was home to a number of birds and squirrels. I kept calling the probation officer to let her know where I was. She wasn't worried about me at all. I didn't want to go back to jail and was housed with a hellish woman that took a lot of restraint.

It was not long before the checks came from FEMA. I was brought to the bank by Tina. The bank said my license was expired to long ago and would not let me open an account. Tina refused to give up. She accompanied me to JD Bank, the clerk called for approval and as she spoke to another party she said, "Are we going to let this slide?" She was referring to me not having a valid ID. This clerk was compassionate realizing a Hurricane had just struck she opened the account. Tina always had a way with working out situations she was so suited for her job.

Up until the hurricane, I was receiving daily mental health treatment at Lake Charles Mental Health. The damage to that building caused us to move to the Volunteers of America. Even though I had money, I continued to look through the trash bins for clothes. I found several pairs of black pants and a green Victoria Secrets bra. I was glad to find a pair of sneakers.

I was introduced to Karla who was in charge of job skills for the clients of Volunteers of America. I went through the motions of making a resume but I knew no one would hire me and I filled out job applications.

One day we came in and were told Karla died of a brain amorism, she was only 24 years old. Now another worker takes over helping us find jobs. One day, she called me to ask me to go to a disability job fair. I started to say no but then realized I'm not doing anything and I don't have any money. My roommate and me went together and filled out applications. When I got to Kroger's I filled out the application and was hired. The hiring manager said report to the store at 10:00 am for drug testing. I went by bus and was drug tested and given a schedule. I doubted myself that I could keep up with this job. I had no transportation. I was mentally ill for God's sake. All kinds of questions went through my mind. How will I get to work? What do I do if I am scheduled at night?

My caseworker told me they will not provide transportation. I made up my mind that I would walk. If I put one foot in front of the other I would move forward.

I walked two miles to work and two miles home. I worked about 25 hours per week. My feet and legs hurt from years of no exercise. I was determined to earn money. I never touched my money in the bank for cab fare or any kind of car.

News came from Volunteers of America that we were going to move. I was moved to a two bedroom apartment to live alone. My roommate demanded to see my apartment and complained that I had a better place. I was so grateful I did not have to live with this abusive e woman any more. I left work and caught the bus home. I was so worried that the new place would be a problem getting to and from work. I asked the bus driver how to get to my street. Giovanni Street he said, it's a straight shot through the projects. I walked with no idea where I was going when I saw Lake Street and JT's Seafood. I was so happy it was only a few blocks from the bus stop.

The apartment had been furnished with an old scratched up furniture and old mattress.

I asked Tina to bring me to get furniture. I should have just got a twin bed and dresser. I bought a queen size bed which took up to much of the room. I bought a sofa and cocktail table with night stands from Home Furniture. I installed a phone and cable. Most important I cherished my job and would be able to get to and from it by bus.

While my former roommate drank herself to sleep at night, I fell asleep from being tired. At 5 am I was awakened by a knock. It was my probation officer. I was like I am home every night and I do not go out except to go to work.

As time went on I was called to the office of Kroger's manager. He said, I'm not going to let some little old slowest cashier in America ruin my production numbers. Your too slow now what do you have to say? I responded, "I'm not quitting." The manager said, you're going to make me go through the counseling calling you up here. I responded, do what you got to do. I went downstairs crying but I was still employed.

As time went on I topped production as a cashier and made it to supervisor. I also began working the Customer Service Booth.

When it was time to file taxes I looked forward to receiving my income tax refund. The tax refund was garnished by the Louisiana tax office for nonpayment of student loans. I sat out to fix this. I contacted the state and worked out an arrangement that would remove the default from my credit record. It was through a collection agency.

As time went on I deferred the student loan and felt that I had almost completed the Paralegal program and applied for admission to the university. They accepted me and I worked almost full time and went to school full time.

I endured a host of reminding customers and employees who talked about me and my crime spree. I endure it determined to alter the future that man had laid out for me to fail. The crime spree made the front page and my acquittal made the front page. It was on news cast on the national level. The whole time I was incarcerated I devoted my whole time to God and reading my bible. I prayed and I participated in the choir. There were mail bible studies such as Stone croft, Berea Prison Ministries and Crossroads Bible Institute. Even after being released I participated in Crossroad Bible Institute studies.

CHAPTER 7

The Crime Spree

I DIDN'T NEED people reminding me of what I did. I felt bad enough. Some people thought I should move and I thought that I should stay. They made comments like why should we live in fear. That comment made me fear retaliation for going free. One of the comments I heard frequently was why you give her a job she shot her brother, I need a job, why you don't give me a job.

At first, it hurt deeply but then I sat down and thought about that time and that day. I walked away from the crime scene at the service center. There were spectators, a man walking a baby. My aunt and cousins and various everyday people were trying to get my attention. I walked pass the dismal houses and observed a man sitting lifeless on the porch. The police car turned on the same street I was on and stopped. I placed my hands on the back of my head and just waited for him. He got out of the police car about 20 feet away with his gun out; he says I'm not going to shoot you. He placed my hands on the car and searched my purse. One of my friends once told me, the human brain is never blank. Well, my brain was void of thought. I looked at my Aunt hollering in front of her home. I was place in handcuffs and placed in the car. He read me my rights and the officer drove me back to the scene of the crime.

It was complete chaos multiple police cars and ambulances. I could see the victims' families hugging and expressing that they had survived. I remember glaring at James because he was the man I wanted to shoot. I saw the woman I shot on a gurney at the time I did not know who she was. All the victims were receiving help from the first responders. My thoughts were wondering if they were dead. I was placed in the police car my rights read to me again. I had never been arrested before so this experience was a shock that I was even capable of what I just did. I didn't think about bond, about family, nor did I ever expect to go free. My last stop before being in prison for the rest of my life was this gloomy place. The officer tried to talk to me but I couldn't talk and was still in handcuffs when I was led to the booking room from the back of the police station.

I encountered a female police officer. She asked me questions and I responded it was me. I began to follow her instruction and I watched her face for expression there was none. I gave my name and personal information. I was placed in a small cell which coasted of a toilet, a slab for a bed. It was cold and I unfolded the blanket and rolled up on the slab and went to sleep. I could see through my partially opened eyes a police officer just standing there. He didn't say anything to me and wide eyed I just looked up at him as he calmly walked off. There appeared to be some activity going on. Another officer rushed by and said doesn't wash your hands. I thought about the contents of my purse where I shoved my gardening gloves and the gun. I felt an undeserved relief because there will be no residue on my hands. The residue would be on my garden gloves.

The Sergeant came to the cell and asked if he could get me anything, he suggested coffee. I said yes, but the coffee never came. I was lead to the interrogation room where I folded my arms and let them envelop my head. The first detective came in and whatever he said I don't remember. We did not talk. For some reason he yelled, turn out. What the hell, I was not processing anything that was going on. The second detective came in after the first one left, He sat calmly at the table with me and he says nothing. Our silence was interrupted by the Sergeant who never made good on his coffee offer. He said tell me about the fire, I was silent, but not completely out of my body. We found your brother dead and we think you had something to do with it. I stilled remained silent while he produced documents for me to initial and sign. In my state of mind I was just initialing and signing papers I did not know what I was signing. I was thinking I'm guilty I did this and I am going to prison for the rest of my life. I wasn't aware enough to ask for an attorney. The Sergeant read me my rights, charged me and I was transported to the Calcasieu Corrections Center.

I wanted to tell them how I was thinking about my brother; I shot, at the time. How he kicked in the door and said he was a hit man for the Sheriff's office. Then later confided, two deputies told him he could be a hit man for the Sheriff's. This caused for me to file and internal affairs report with the Sheriff's Office. He brought prostitutes into the backroom of my mother's house. He would not allow her rides on certain times or brought my mother places and just left her. How he fits of hollering and cutting up to get her to buy, cigarettes, beer, or gas. I wanted to say that night was the night he planned to do something. He came in and out of the house all night. He was by my window and the window fell breaking the glass. I felt I was a victim long before I had victims. I couldn't talk and I felt like I did it and it didn't matter what I said. I was here now and I was never going home again.

I knew very little about jails and prisons. I would sometimes bring money orders to place money on the accounts of my younger brother. Then on other occasions to have them pick up my brother for psychiatric services, they called it an OPC. Other than those situations, I had no connection. I applied once and they set me up for a test. I did not show up because I had mental illness and who was I kidding. I couldn't do this job.

I was booked into jail. I had no middle name and to this day the jail keep sticking me with a middle name. I never talked to any more detectives. I had a problem getting an attorney. At first it was Ron Ware, I began to tell him what happened, I tried to lie and say Pete was asleep. He was not asleep when I shot him, he was laying down and when the first shot rang out he sat up and I shot him again. He said, Kooey, for some reason. Maybe something he saw. But I stopped when I realized I could not lie my way out of my situation. He set up an appointment to be evaluated by a psychiatrist. I felt uncomfortable with my attorney because it seemed like I had some personal dealings with him when I was in my late teens. I could not remember so I ask John to help me recuse him. He was recused and a conflicts attorney was appointed. After all, it was Eugene Bouquet.

I was brought to a psychiatrist. She asked me what happened. I told her my ex-husband abused me and I divorced. He kept messing with me and then filed for custody of my kids. He got custody then he asked me for child support even though he earned $70,000 a year. I was not working and attending college. He kept messing with me. His brother helped him get custody of our kids by allowing my daughter who frequently stayed with them to get a plane ticket to Pennsylvania. Also, allowing my daughter to talk to my ex-husband without me knowing or monitoring their conversations. She spent every weekend with my former in laws and although his family never gave a birthday card or gift to them their entire lives or visited our home in Baton Rouge, they all had something to say when I got custody. They did not love my kids like I loved my children. I breastfed my kids and was very involved with their lives in spite of my mental illness which was diagnosed in 1988. He served me with papers to pay child support knowing I could not afford an attorney and represented myself. The judge gave an elaborate custody plan with me flying the kid's home 3 or 4 times a year.

The psychiatrist asked me what happened with your brother. My brother wanted to kill us. My younger brother came to me in my bedroom and told me our brother asked him to kill my mother. I was stunned that he would have the audacity to want to kill my mother. He said he thinks we were trying to put him out of the house. I picked my mother with questions why he would think we were trying to put him out the house. She had evicted him from the house and the police evicted him. The charges of trespassing came back up after 3 years and he was being summoned to court. He came back to live in her house and when the police were called they did not come. I moved in with my kids after this. I was standing in the kitchen and witnessed my brother talking to himself saying what he was going to do about Lizabeth. He gave me a ride and while in the car he started masturbating in front of me. He drove his car almost 100 miles per hour down Jackson Street, one time. I was getting him help by going to the coroner for Orders of Protective Custody's but the doctor said to get him some permanent help. He was suggesting interdiction which we could not afford. I told my story over and over to doctor after doctor. I was always telling it with the knowledge I'm going to prison for the rest of my life. I went before the Sanity Commission who said I should not be released from jail without a mental health treatment plan. The Courts did more than that, they made sure I got mental health, a place to live, and those caseworkers tried to get me disability. I held on to whatever was working. I told them how my ex-husband abused me, that making love was like being raped. That we loved our children and our problems were not with the beautiful children we had. The problem was our relationship him feeling the need to cut me down in front of other people, what he said. The arguing, when he knew his family told him he would never make it. The job he got when we were together he still has. Deep down I was afraid of my husband, I was afraid for my children and I felt he would harm them. This hurt me but I could not help the situation so I enrolled in college and he still kept coming after me. I just wanted to be left alone. I was angry at them. But grateful they were so abusive they got on TV saying that thang is crazy, Because of them the insanity plea was being ordered. The Sanity Commission spoke and the Judge made a decision for me to be released to a home. That housing situation never transpired.

I woke up imprisoned, we ate breakfast and I told my praying inmates, I'm going to court will you join me in prayer. We formed a circle and everyone was believing on a victory. I am called and brought to court. Judge Painter finds me Not Guilty by Reason of Insanity and approves the Conditional Release. The District Attorney that agreed to the insanity defense died of a heart attack. I returned to the dormitory holding the yellow paper high in the air. Someone asked how did it go, I said Not Guilty, they clapped and congratulated me. I could not contain myself.

What happened next was a shame before Jesus Christ. I was held for one year and 10 months and during that time I prayed. I prayed more and I asked him to please work it out. All the women I had been incarcerated with came and went. One day it was time for class and the Mentor did not come. Another inmate and I asked the deputies if we could proceed and they said yes. She and I chose the scripture 1 Samuel. I told them how Hannah was vexed in her spirit because she could not bear children. She went to God and she vowed that it if he gave her a son she would dedicate that son to him and let him be his servant. She became pregnant and she followed up with that vow to God. Following Hannah's example, I am telling you all that when I leave this jail I'm coming back to let you all know that you can break the cycle of jail. You can beat the game out there on the streets.

The year is now 2020; it's been 19 years since I made the biggest mistake of my life. I had asked Crossroad Bible Institute to be a Mentor correcting questionnaires they sent inmates in the mail. Also, writing a letters to prisoners. I had to have my priest sign the application. The Deacon read what I had written I would say to offenders in prison. He forwarded it to other organizations. I received a call from a lady with The Open Door Ministry. She called and asked if I would be interested in working with her organization. I was thrilled. I told her specifically I would be interested in Life Skills and Reentry classes. She opened that door for me and to this date I am a facilitator teaching Life Skills and Reentry at the Calcasieu Corrections Women's Prison. I went on to becoming a full time clerk for Kroger's earning more than I would if I worked in my field. I have been with Kroger's for 15 years. I went back to college and earned a Bachelor's Degree in General Studies with concentration in Behavioral Sciences and also and Associates of Arts degree in Paralegal Studies. After 12 years the Judge in my case released me from probation. I live in a small apartment and I am comfortable. I'm not in prison and I thank almighty God for that. I am an example of God's love. What he could do for you and to you if you just believe.

CHAPTER 8

2020

I DON'T KNOW if I fit a profile of a killer. I certainly didn't have an ordinary life. I was the eighth child of nine children. We all looked alike or resembled. We all had accomplishments from the oldest to the youngest. Each one with their own talent and each of us playing every day in the school playground and surrounded by friends all the time. I always had friends and one of them was a deputy on duty who I had teased about being tall. I had school mates who were policemen and deputies. I did consider law enforcement as a career and the army too. That ship never sailed for me instead I joined the millions of people watching crime shows on TV.

When the government integrated schools I joined my school mates and was bussed to Pearl Watson Junior High. I didn't see white people as being any different from us so I did not have a problem with race. I tried out for track and enjoyed being a runner. Then, I heard about cheerleading and gave that a shot. I was elected and I loved it. I didn't make it when I got to Lake Charles High School my first tryout but I did make it, senior year. I loved it. I loved making my body flip and flop and jump as high as I could go. I loved my co cheerleaders. The other black senior was not athletic as I was but I watched as she fit right in and her little muscles started to bulge. We would walk home after practice and just talk. It was a time when we did not have to fear being abducted or assaulted by just walking the street. I played basketball in high school and I was generally outgoing. I still felt alone with all my family woes and problems. My dad abandoned us during the highlight of my life. But I got through it and now I think about all the scriptures that made me realize that I got through some of the worst times in anybody's life. If God will bring you to it, he will bring you through it. He did too. In Romans it has so many encouraging scriptures. We are all sinners and fall short of the glory of God. As each lay minister belted out scripture after scripture I got stronger and stronger. God prepared me to journey to this point of writing this book. It seems over time I had to learn of his grace and mercy. That without Him I am nothing. I was nothing, a void, depressed and weeping all the time. Now, I am alive and with courage and strength. I am able to talk about my life and what hurt me without feeling shame. I feel remorse and I cry but it's not every day. It's only on occasion. My typical day, I get up, I get coffee and I shower up and clean myself up. I arrive at work usually within a half hour of my cleaning ritual. I have a variety of duties. Currently I am a supervisor. I was a Certified Receiver and that job I loved but I did not get along with my coworker. I asked to be moved and I landed back on the front end. When I get home, I cook and I have a few beers. Then, I get undressed and fall blissfully to sleep. They say the wicked never sleep so I assume I am not the wicked they speak about. I don't think I am a bad person or a person you should avoid. I made a mistake. The mistake that no one should dare make. The taking of a life is a horrible way to go. If you think you can just cop a plea and get off with murder, you can't. According to what I was taught, an insanity plea is the most difficult pleas to prove. There are defenses such as self-defense but you still have to have proof. There are too many people falling into the trap of violent crime and spending years in prison. If you ask me, I would say don't ever do it. Jail is just a cage and it is inhumane. I won't say I grew a pair of balls in jail, but I toughened up and things such as passing gas in public seem so minor. I was so self-conscious before I landed in jail that I lost all the self-consciousness.

I found the courage to sue the Community Forensic worker in federal court for having me arrested in 2016 without cause. She claimed I missed a meeting on June 3, 2016 but I was arrested on May 27, 2016, she was defended by the State of Louisiana and I represented myself. The judge ruled she had qualified immunity. I contended she acted outside the scope of her duties. I felt because I was a black female I was held in the system instead of being released after 5 years. She never cited anything dangerous I was doing other than she was scared of me.

When I talk to female inmates at the jail, my first question is does anyone recognize me. Surprising one or two have remembered me from my days in jail. I try to talk to them about being entrapped in the system. I am surprised that very few African Americans take my class at the jail. I have said many times to our mentees, the person who turned you on to drugs knew you would get addicted. They knew once you were addicted, you would do anything for drugs. They knew you would steal, they knew you would prostitute, they knew you would rob somebody, they knew you would forge checks, steal credit cards, they knew you would shoplift and they knew you would even take a charge for them. Some of you have charges and you serve your time only to have to come right back to jail on charges that were already on the books. For some of you jail is a revolving door, you leave and come right back. You can free yourself from this cycle but you have pray for help. God will see you through the rough patches. He will make a way out of no way. I encourage you to read your bible and trust and believe God can set you free.

My favorite songs in prison ministry is Jesus Will Fix It, Jesus Can Work It Out, Jesus On The Mainline, This Little Light Of Mine, I'm Looking For A Miracle, God Kept Me, Everything That Happened To Me That Was Good, God Did It, Oh Give Thanks. I leave my readers with this scripture, 1st John4: 7-21 and ask that you pray for love, for love conquer all.

9 781984 588661